The Christmas Dinner

BY

SHEPHERD KNAPP

[ZHINGOORA BOOKS]

This edition is published by
Zhingoora Books.

The Cover is Designed by Pallav Sethiya.

Preface

This play is intended, not only for acting, but also for reading. It is so arranged that boys and girls can read it to themselves, just as they would read any other story. Even the stage directions and the descriptions of scenery are presented as a part of the narrative. At the same time, by the use of different styles of type, the speeches of the characters are clearly distinguished from the rest of the text, an arrangement which will be found convenient when parts are being memorized for acting.

The play has been acted more than once, and by different groups of people; sometimes on a stage equipped with footlights, curtain, and scenery; sometimes with barely any of these aids. Practical suggestions as to costumes, scenery, and some simple scenic effects will be found at the end of the play.

What sort of a Christmas play do the boys and girls like, and in what sort do we like to see them take part? It should be a play, surely, in which the dialogue is simple and natural, not stilted and artificial; one that seems like a bit of real life, and yet has plenty of fancy and imagination in it; one that suggests and helps to perpetuate some of the happy and wholesome customs of Christmas; above all, one that is pervaded by the Christmas spirit. I hope that this play does not entirely fail to meet these requirements.

Worcester, Mass.

SHEPHERD KNAPP.

Before the Play begins, MOTHER GOOSE comes out in front of the curtain, and this is what she says:

Well, well, well, well, well, here we all are again. And what's more important, Christmas is here again, too. Aren't you glad? Now I want to tell you children something. Do you know what I enjoy most at Christmas time? It's to come in here and see all you children sitting in rows and rows, all your faces looking up at me, and a smile on every one of them. Why, even some of those great big men and women back there are smiling, too. And I think I know why you are all smiling. There are two reasons for it, I believe. One is that you think old Mother Goose is a good friend of yours, and loves you all very much. And you're quite right about that, for I declare, I love every one of you as much as I love—plum pudding. And the second reason why you are all smiling, I guess, is because you think I am going to show you a Christmas Play. And you're right about that, too. I have a play all ready for you, there behind the curtain, and the name of it is "The Christmas Dinner." Doesn't the very name of it make you hungry? Well, you just wait. Now when the curtain opens, you'll see the warm cozy kitchen of a farm house, where six people live. Two of them are quite young, because they are just a boy and a girl, and their names are Walter and Gertrude. And two of them are older, and yet not so very old either: they are the father and mother of the two children. And the last two are the oldest of all, and they are *really* old, for they are the children's grandfather and grandmother. It is late in the afternoon of the day before Christmas, the hour when it has begun to get dark. The father is out cutting some good big sticks of wood for the Christmas fire, and the two children are playing outside of the house. So you'll not see them at first. But you will see the mother, who is just finishing the day's work, and the old grandfather and grandmother, who are sitting by the fire. Are you ready, all of you? Be quiet, then, for now it is going to begin.

The Christmas Dinner

The First Scene

Now the Curtain opens, and you see a farmhouse kitchen, just as Mother Goose promised. At the back, opposite to you, is a fire-place, with a mantel shelf over it. A bright fire is burning. On the mantel is a lamp, lighted, and an unlighted candle; also some other things that you'll hear about later. There is a cupboard against the back wall. At one side of the room is the door leading out of doors; beside it is a large wood box, where the fire-wood is kept; and nearby are a broom, leaning against the wall, and a dustpan. On the other side of the room is another door, which leads to the rest of the house; beside that is a big clothes basket, where the soiled clothes are kept. Close to the fire, one on each side, the Grandfather and the Grandmother are sitting in comfortable chairs. Near the front and a little at one side are a table and a chair. On the table is a dishpan and a number of dishes, which the Mother is washing when the curtain opens.

The first one to speak is the GRANDMOTHER, *and this is what she says:* Haven't you nearly finished, Mary?

Yes, almost, *answers* MOTHER: only a few more things to be washed, and then I can sit down and rest.

GRANDMOTHER *asks,* Is everything ready for the Christmas dinner tomorrow?

Every single thing, MOTHER answers. The goose is ready to go on the fire; the apple sauce is made; the bread and the pies are baked; and the plum pudding—well, you saw the pudding yourself, so that I don't need to tell you about that. It's a beauty, if I do say so.

At this moment the outside door opens, and the two children, Walter and Gertrude, run in. Their coats and mittens show that they have been playing in the snow.

Oh, Mother, says WALTER, it's getting dark outside. May we come in now? Is your work all done?

Not quite yet, dears, *his* MOTHER answers. Run out, both of you, for ten minutes more, and then I'll have everything cleared away. It makes me nervous to have you about while things are in a mess.

All right, mother, *says* GERTRUDE. Come on, Walter, I'll race you to the gate. *And both the children go out-of-doors again, running. Gertrude was nearer the door, and gets out first.*

Such energy as those children have! *exclaims* MOTHER, *with a sigh, as she goes on with her work.* Sometimes it makes me tired to watch them. There, every last thing is washed, and now, when I've dried them, I can sit down. *She goes on talking while she dries.* There's one thing I haven't had time to do—those paper caps. I suppose the children will be disappointed, but I simply couldn't find time to make them. The colored paper and paste and scissors are all on the mantel shelf and I suppose I ought to sit right down now and go to work on them, but I declare, I'm too tired. Getting ready for Christmas seems to take all the strength I have. I think I must be getting old.

You getting old! *exclaims GRANDMOTHER. Nonsense! Wait till you get to be our age; then you might talk of getting old and feeling tired. Isn't that so, John?* John is Grandfather's first name.

Yes, GRANDFATHER *answers,* when you get to be as old as we are, then you'll know what it is to be tired, Christmas or another day. I tried to help James shut the gate this morning, where the snow had drifted against it, and it tired me so, I haven't stirred out of this chair since.

Now the outside door opens a second time, and the children come in again, Gertrude first.

Isn't it time now, mother? *asks GERTRUDE.*

Yes, *answers MOTHER,* I've just finished. Take off your coats, and try to quiet down. *She puts the clean dishes away in the cupboard and carries the dish pan away into the next room.*

The children take of their coats and caps. Walter goes over by his Grandfather and leans against his chair. Gertrude sits down on a low stool beside her Grandmother.

What have you children been doing all the afternoon? *asks GRANDFATHER.*

Oh, we've had the greatest fun, *cries GERTRUDE.* First we went skating down on the mill pond.

And then we built a snow fort, WALTER *chimes in*, and the Indians attacked it, and we drove them off with snow-balls.

And then we played tag out by the barn, *adds* GERTRUDE.

No, WALTER *corrects her*, that was afterwards; don't you remember, Gertrude? Before that, we raced down to the crossroads to see if the postman had brought any mail.

Oh, yes, GERTRUDE *agrees*, and you tripped and fell down in the snow drift, and oh, grandfather, you ought to have seen him when he got up; he was a sight. But it all brushed off.

And don't you feel tired after doing all that? GRANDMOTHER *asks*.

No, *says* GERTRUDE, I'm not a bit tired; are you, Walter?

Not a bit, *says* WALTER.

Well, that's the beauty of being young, GRANDMOTHER *says, in a tired sort of voice.* I suppose that when I was your age, I was just the same as you children are now.

How long is it since you were our age? WALTER *asks*.

So many years, *says* GRANDMOTHER, that I haven't time to count them up. But I can remember it all clearly enough, even if it was so long ago. Everything about it was very different then from the way it is now.

How was it different, grandmother? *asks* GERTRUDE.

Why, in all sorts of ways, GRANDMOTHER answers. For one thing, the days seemed ever so much shorter when I was a little girl.

And the nights, adds GRANDFATHER. Nowadays the nights are sometimes quite long, but when I was a boy they were so short, that it almost seemed as though there weren't any nights at all.

And food used to taste quite different then, says GRANDMOTHER. I used to care a lot more for breakfast and dinner and supper then than I do now.

Grandfather, asks WALTER, do you wish that you could have stayed on being a little boy, always?

Well, I don't know, Walter, GRANDFATHER replies thoughtfully; there are two sides to that. I'll tell you what I would like, though. I'd like to be a little boy now and then, just for a short time, to see once more how it would feel to run and shout and play and eat and laugh, the way I used to. But then I think I'd pretty soon want to be myself again, old as I am, because there are some grand things about old age that I think I'd miss if I had to be a little boy for good and all. A good many wonderful things happen to you when you grow old, and even if my old body does get pretty tired sometimes, and you children think perhaps that grandfather looks very stupid, sitting so quiet by the fire-side here, I'm often thinking, inside, of splendid things that little boys and girls don't know anything about.

But, grandfather, says GERTRUDE, tell us some more things that were different when you were a boy.

Well, let me see, GRANDFATHER *says, and stops for a moment to think. Then he goes on.* There were the brownies. I haven't said anything about them, have I?

The brownies? *exclaims* WALTER, *his eyes big with interest.* What about the brownies?

Only that when I was a little boy, *answers* GRANDFATHER, I used to see the brownies sometimes. But now I never see them. It's many a long year since I caught sight of a single one.

Where did you used to see them? *asks* WALTER, *still excited.*

Right here in this room, *answers* GRANDFATHER. There used to be two of them, when I was a boy; and often I would see them, though none of the grown-up people could see them at all. During the daytime they used often to hide in the wood-box over there: and then at night, they used to come out and play. And sometimes they worked, too, for I can remember my father saying sometimes in the morning, "The floor looks so clean that I think the brownies must have swept it last night."

But, Grandfather, *says* WALTER, *for there is one thing about this that puzzles him,* I'm a little boy, and I've never seen the brownies.

No, not yet, GRANDFATHER *admits,* but I think you're likely to any time now. You see, they don't show themselves to very little boys, for fear of frightening them.

GERTRUDE, *who has been listening carefully to all of this, has a question to ask.* Grandmother, *she says,* did you see the brownies, too, when you were a little girl?

No, indeed, *answers* GRANDMOTHER. The brownies never wanted any girls to see them. But I used to see the house-fairies often, and *they* always hid away from the *boys,* so that only we girls ever saw *them.*

How many house-fairies were there, Grandmother, *asks* GERTRUDE *eagerly,* and where did you see them, and what did they do?

My, what a lot of questions! GRANDMOTHER *says, smiling at Gertrude's excitement.* There were two of them at our house, and they lived in the kitchen just as the brownies did here. They used to hide in a big clothes basket very much like that one over there. At night, like the brownies, they used to do some of the house-work to help mother; and how pleased she used to be, when she found in the morning that some of the work had been done for her while she was asleep.

Do you suppose, *says* WALTER, that if I woke up some night, and came and looked in here, I'd see the brownies working or playing?

Very likely, *answers* GRANDFATHER.

Oh, I'd like to try it, *cries* WALTER. Can I do it tonight?

But GRANDMOTHER *says:* No, indeed, Walter. What is your Grandfather thinking of to put such a notion into your head. And as for tonight—well, of all nights in the year!—the very night when we expect Santa Claus to come and fill the stockings. And you know how displeased he would be to find the children awake and watching him. Why, he very likely would go away without leaving a single present.

To be sure, *says GRANDFATHER*. No, it wouldn't do at all. And, besides, think how tired you'd be for tomorrow. And *then* you'd be sorry with all the goings-on. By dinner time, you'd probably be falling asleep, and we'd have to eat all the goose and the pudding without you.

We wouldn't want to miss that, *says GERTRUDE, shaking her head decisively*. I saw the pudding out in the store closet, and I tell you, it smelt good.

I bet you tasted it, *exclaims WALTER*.

Indeed I did not, *answers GERTRUDE in a hurt tone;* not even the eentiest teentiest bit of it.

What time will the dinner begin, grandfather? *asks WALTER*.

About twelve o'clock noon, I expect, *GRANDFATHER answers*.

And I suppose, *says WALTER in a sorrowful voice,* that the pudding will be the last thing of all.

Yes, I suppose so, *GRANDFATHER admits*.

It will be an awfully long time to wait, *says WALTER*. And then when mother begins to help it, Gertrude and I will have to wait and wait while all the rest of you are helped. It's pretty tiresome waiting sometimes.

But have you forgotten, Walter? GRANDMOTHER *says, reminding him,* You won't have to wait as long as that tomorrow. For tomorrow is Christmas, and don't you remember, that one of the ways in which Christmas is different from all the other days in the year, is the way in which the food is helped out at the Christmas dinner? On other days the oldest people are helped first, and the youngest ones have to wait: but at Christmas dinner, the first one to be helped to each thing is the very youngest one of all, and then comes the next youngest, and so on all the way round, and the oldest one has to wait till the very last.

Oh, I remember, *exclaims* GERTRUDE. That was the way we did last year. Don't you remember, Walter? *Walter nods.* And last year, GERTRUDE *goes on,* I was the youngest and I was helped first to every single thing. Grandmother, who is the youngest this year?

Why, you are the youngest, *answers* GRANDMOTHER, just as you were last Christmas.

But I'm a whole year older than I was then, *says* GERTRUDE, *looking puzzled.*

And so is everybody else, GRANDMOTHER *explains.*

Really? *says* GERTRUDE, *not quite convinced.* So I'm the youngest still? Will I be helped first to the goose and the apple sauce?

Yes, *answers GRANDMOTHER.*

And will she be helped first to the pudding,
too? *asks WALTER anxiously.*

Yes, *answers GRANDMOTHER.*

Oh, I'm so glad, *cries GERTRUDE.* Isn't it nice to be the youngest?

Am I the next youngest? *asks WALTER.*

Yes, GRANDMOTHER *answers,* and the second helping of
everything will go to you.

Oh, well, that's all right, *says WALTER, a good deal relieved.*
There's sure to be plenty left. Gertrude couldn't eat it all.

*Now there is the sound of someone outside the door, stamping to
shake the snow from his boots.*

There's Father, *cries GERTRUDE. She and Walter go to the door
and open it. Their father comes in, carrying several good-sized
pieces fire-wood.*

How late you are, James, *says GRANDFATHER,* and how tired
you look.

I am tired, *answers FATHER. He lifts the lid of the wood-box, and
throws in the wood with a great clatter. Then, while he takes off his
cap and gloves and muffler, he says:* The snow is so deep that it's
hard to walk in it, especially carrying a load as heavy as that
wood was. *He sits down.*

Children, *says* GRANDMOTHER, go, tell your mother that father is here. She'll want to give us supper at once and hurry you both off to bed.

But when are we to hang up our stockings? *asks* WALTER.

We'll do that right after supper, *answers* FATHER. Run along now, and tell mother that I'm here. *The children go, and* FATHER *continues speaking.* Is everything all ready for tomorrow? *he asks.*

Yes, *answers* GRANDMOTHER, Mary finished everything quite a while ago. Or almost everything. She didn't get the paper caps made for the children, but she was just too tired to do it after all the other work.

I don't wonder, *says* FATHER. When there is so much to be done, some things simply have to be left. Perhaps there will be time tomorrow morning. I'm leaving some things for tomorrow myself. For instance, I promised Mary I'd sweep out the kitchen here, after I'd brought in the wood; and it needs it, sure enough, for I see I've tracked in a lot of dirt. But I'm going to beg off for tonight. I'll do it first thing in the morning. I only hope that Santa Claus won't notice it, and think we're an untidy household. But we leave such a dim light in the kitchen at night, that I don't believe he'll be able to tell whether the room is broom-clean or not. And any way, I guess he must get tired himself sometimes. So he'll know how it is, and won't lay it up against us.

And that is the end of the First Scene.

The Interlude

Again before the Second Scene begins, MOTHER GOOSE comes out in front of the Curtain, and this is what she says:

Children, do you want to know what has happened in that Kitchen since the curtain closed? Well, I've come to tell you all about it. The first thing was that they all had supper; not a very hearty supper, because they all wanted to save up their appetites for the Christmas dinner the next day. But they had as much as they needed. And then the two children went and got their stockings, one for each member of the family, and then they all hung up their own stockings. Gertrude hung up her stocking, and Walter hung up his stocking, and Mother hung up her stocking, and Father hung up his stocking, and Grandmother hung up her stocking, and—and—and—now, I declare, I've left somebody out. Who can it be, I wonder? Why, to be sure—Grandfather. Yes, Grandfather hung up his stocking; and there they were, all six stockings hanging in a row. You look for them there, when the curtain opens. I think you'll see them. Well, then of course the children went to bed, and by this time I think they are both asleep. And now the rest of the family are beginning to feel sleepy, and in just a moment, I think one of them is going to say, "It's time we *all* went to bed." What happens after that you can see for yourselves, for now it's going to begin.

The Second Scene

When the Curtain opens, you see the Kitchen again just as before, except that now the six stockings are hanging from the mantel shelf over the fire-place. Father is sitting beside the table reading the newspaper. The two Grandparents are still sitting close to the fire, one on each side. Grandfather has fallen asleep, and Grandmother is drowsy, so that her head nods. Then she wakes up, and tries to stay awake; but in a minute her head goes nodding again. Father yawns, puts down his newspaper; yawns once more and stretches; then goes on reading.

MOTHER *comes in and says,* The children are sound asleep.

It's time we all went to bed, *says* FATHER, *putting down the newspaper.* I know I'm ready for it. *He yawns.*

Besides, *adds* MOTHER, the fire is almost out; and indeed it ought soon to be put out entirely, so as to cool the chimney for old Santa Claus, when he comes.

That's right, too, FATHER *agrees. He gets up and goes to Grandfather, laying his hand on his shoulder.* Father, *he says, speaking loud so as to waken him.* It's time to go to bed.

What? *says* GRANDFATHER, *waking up with a start; and then he says,* Why, I must have been dozing. Where are the children?

They went to bed long ago, *says* MOTHER. Don't you remember? And now it's bed time for all of us. Are you ready, mother?

Yes, I'm more than ready, answers GRANDMOTHER. She rises and Grandfather, also, and with feeble steps, they go toward the door. Good-night, GRANDMOTHER says.

Good-night, FATHER and MOTHER answer her, and FATHER continues, Good-night, father. Pleasant dreams.

Good-night, answers GRANDFATHER, and he and Grandmother go out.

I'll be off too, James, says MOTHER, if you'll look after the fire and the light.

Yes, I'll attend to all that, answers FATHER.

Then Mother goes out, and Father deadens the fire, using the tongs and shovel. He takes the chair, in which he has been sitting, and sets it against the wall beside the clothes basket. Then he lights the candle on the mantel shelf, blows out the lamp, leaving the room in a dim light, and goes out.

For a little while everything is quiet. Then there is a noise from the direction of the wood box. The cover rises, and the head of a brownie appears, inside the box. He climbs out, followed by another. They caper about the room, looking at everything, listening at the doors, looking up the chimney. Then they go to the clothes basket and raise the lid. Up come four arms, and then two house-fairies stand up in the basket, and get out with the help of the chair. They, also, flit about the room, looking at things. Meanwhile the brownies have taken the broom and dust pan, and begun to sweep, especially over by the outside door and by the wood box. The fairies take a chair, and climb up by the mantel shelf. They take down the colored paper, paste and scissors, and, carrying them to the table, set to work, making paper caps. In a few moments they hold up two, complete. They leave them on the table.

Now sleigh bells are heard approaching. The brownies and fairies leave their work, and clapping their hands, run to the fire-place, and stand in a group, facing it, looking in. Now the sleigh bells have come very near: and now they are still. And NOW Santa Claus is heard scrambling down the chimney. As he comes out from the fire-place, the brownies and fairies separate to let him through. He sets down his pack. Then the brownies, on one side, and the fairies, on the other, take hold of his hands and draw him toward the front of the stage.

SANTA CLAUS smiles down at them, and, shaking the hands that hold his, says, How are you all? Merry as crickets? They nod, and dance up and down, still holding his hands. And what have you been doing with yourselves? he asks them. Playing? They all nod. And working? he asks. They nod again. Then the brownies draw him over to the their side, and show him how clean the floor is. Good! says SANTA CLAUS. Then the brownies let go his hand, and the fairies draw him over to their side, and show him the caps they have made. Fine! says SANTA CLAUS. Then the fairies let go his other hand, and he goes on talking. How are Gertrude and Walter? Have they been good? They all nod. As for the older people, he says, I don't need to ask you about them. Do you want to know why? They nod. It's because I've heard all about them already, SANTA CLAUS continues. There's a little bird that lives up in the eaves of the house and often he flies down and listens at the window, and then he tells me all he hears. Tonight he flew way up to the pine woods on the hill, to meet me, and he told me some things about all the older people in this house which made me feel quite upset. Shall I tell you what it was? *They nod.* He says that they all of them seem to think that they are growing old, not only the grandfather and grandmother, but the father and mother, too. They are all the time talking about feeling tired, and saying how different it all was when they were children, and how long ago that seems. Now isn't that a shame? I don't blame them altogether, because I know myself how that sort of thing sometimes happens. Two or three years ago I was sick for awhile, and I declare that even I began to feel old and tired. But all the same I don't believe in letting that sort of thing go on too long; and do you want to know what I am going to do about it? *They nod eagerly.* It's the best scheme you ever heard of, and I want you to help me with it. Well, I'm going to use some magic to make them all little boys and girls again for half an hour. And the way I'm going to do it is this. I've got here a bag of magic hazel nuts. *He takes the bag out of his pocket.* I always keep them in my pocket, because you never know when a thing of that sort will come in handy. Now, I want you to take these nuts and stick them into the plum pudding, which they are all going to eat tomorrow for their Christmas dinner. You must stick them in all around in different places, so that each of the older people will be sure to get one; and it won't do the children a bit of harm if they get some, too. In fact they are so young that this kind of magic won't have any effect on them at all. But with all the older folks, as soon as the nuts have been eaten, the magic will begin to work; and what do you suppose will be the first thing they will all want to do? Do you want to know? *They all nod.* They will all want to get down on their hands and knees, Grandfather and Grandmother and all, and crawl under the table. Won't that be funny? *They all clap their hands and dance up and down.* That's what the magic hazel nuts will make them

do, *says SANTA CLAUS.* And when they have crawled under the table—you see, it's a table that has a Christmas dinner on it, and that makes a difference, of course—well, when they have crawled under the table, then—. No. I believe I won't tell you about what will happen then. I'll keep it for a surprise and it's something worth seeing you may be sure. So that's the plan. Will you help me? *They all nod most emphatically.* Here are the nuts, then, *he says.* Run and stick them into the pudding, while I fill the stockings.

They take the bag and all run out through the door. Santa Claus goes to the fire-place, and from his pack fills all six stockings. Then, as he finishes and takes up his pack, the brownies and fairies return, and gather round him as he stands in front of the fire-place. SANTA CLAUS says to them, Did you stick them in? *They nod.* All around? *They nod again.* That's right. Well, I'm off. And, tomorrow, if I can manage it, I'm going to come back here at about the time when the nuts begin to work, for I'd like to see the fun myself. Good-bye.

They all shake him by the hand. Then he disappears into the fire-place. They stand in front of it for a moment, and one of the brownies kneels down and looks up the chimney after him. Then sleigh bells are heard on the roof, as the sleigh starts. The brownies and fairies turn around then, and come away from the fire-place.

The brownies run to the wood box, climb in, and pull the lid down over them. At the same time the fairies carry the chair over to the clothes basket, climb onto the chair, step over into the basket, and pull the lid down over them. Then everything is quiet again.

And that is the end of the Second Scene.

The Interlude

Again before the Third Scene begins, MOTHER GOOSE comes out in front of the Curtain, and this is what she says:

Children, I've got a lot to tell you about what has happened to Walter and Gertrude since the curtain closed. For quite a while they went on sleeping, because it was still night, you know. And then morning came, and it didn't take them long to wake up after that, I can tell you. As soon as it was really light, they put on their wrappers, and woke their father and mother, and then they went for the stockings. They took them into their grandparents' room, and Grandmother and Grandfather sat up in bed with shawls over their shoulders, and the rest sat on the edge of the bed. Then they all opened their stockings, and I couldn't begin to tell you what fine presents they found in them, nor how happy they all were. After breakfast they all sat down by the kitchen fire, and father got the big family Bible, and laid it on Grandfather's lap, and Grandfather polished up his spectacles till they shone, and put them on his nose, and then he read about the story of the first Christmas long ago in Bethlehem. And it was all so quiet while he was reading that you could almost hear the snow flakes falling outside, for it had begun to snow. Then, when Grandfather had finished reading, and closed the Bible, they all sang a Christmas carol, which they always sings together every Christmas in that house; and they sang it out so clear and strong, that a traveler in a sleigh, way down at the cross-roads, heard it, and it sounded so good that he stopped his horse in spite of the storm, and listened till it was over. Well, I can't tell you everything else they did that morning except that Father found the floor all swept, and knew it must have been done by the brownies; and then Mother found the paper caps that the house-fairies had made. She was ever so glad; and so were the children when they opened them up and put them on. You'll see how they look on the children's heads when the curtain opens. Then about the dinner. Father had brought in the big table, and set it up in the kitchen in front of the fire-place, and Mother put on the plates and the forks and the knives and the spoons and all the rest. Then the goose was roasted, and, oh, how good it smelt when it was cooking. At last everything was ready and twelve o'clock came, and they all sat down at the table. And do you know, I believe they are still sitting there behind the curtain. But they have finished the goose and the apple sauce and all the good things that went with them, and now they are just going to begin on the pudding. They don't know a thing about the magic nuts, because the brownies and the fairies stuck them in so neatly, that not one of them shows. Mother is just starting to put the pudding on the saucers. I wonder if she will remember about giving it to the youngest first. That's Gertrude, you know. Do you want to see for yourselves whether she remembers? Well, be very quiet then, for now it is going to begin.

The Third Scene

When the Curtain opens, you again see the kitchen, but it looks a good deal different, because the chairs that Grandmother and Grandfather used to sit in have been moved out; so has the small table on which Mother washed the dishes in the First Scene; and now in front of the fire-place is the great big table that Mother Goose told you about. The table cloth on it is so big that it hangs all the way down to the floor. At one end of the table sits Father; then next to him, back of the table facing you, is Grandfather, then Gertrude, then Walter, then Grandmother and at the other end of the table, next to Grandmother, Mother is seated. The children have on those bright-colored paper caps that the house-fairies made. MOTHER, who is helping the pudding, is the first to speak and this is what she says:

There's the first plateful of our Christmas pudding, and that goes to Gertrude, of course. *She hands it to Grandmother, who passes it on to Walter.*

Um! *says WALTER, holding it for a moment under his nose.* That smells good! *He passes it to Gertrude.*

GERTRUDE *asks,* Shall I wait till everybody else is served, before I begin?

No, not today, *says FATHER.* Begin at once. We all want to know how it tastes.

Gertrude tastes it. Oh, it is good, *she says.*

Mother meanwhile has helped another plateful, and passed it to GRANDMOTHER, who says, Walter, here is yours. And she hands it to him. He tastes it.

Is it good, Walter? asks GRANDFATHER.

WALTER with his mouth very full can only say, Um!

Pass this down to Father, says MOTHER, and she starts to hand another plateful of pudding to Grandmother.

Oh, Mother, exclaims GERTRUDE, aren't you younger than Father?

Yes, just by two months, answers MOTHER, keeping the plateful of pudding in her hand. You think I ought to be helped next? All right; we'll keep strictly to the rules, and I'll set this aside for myself, while I help the others. She helps another plateful. This is for you James, she says to Father, and passes it along. And Grandmother, she says, this is for you. She hands a plateful of pudding to Grandmother.

Grandfather, here is yours last of all, because you are the oldest of us, MOTHER says, and starts the last plateful of pudding on its way to Grandfather.

Suddenly FATHER, who has been eating some of his pudding, exclaims, Here's something new. You never put nuts in the plum pudding before, Mary.

Nuts? says MOTHER, very much surprised, There aren't any nuts in the pudding.

But, indeed there are, FATHER insists, I've just eaten one.

And so have I, adds GRANDMOTHER.

And here is another one, declares GRANDFATHER, and he holds it up in his spoon. It's a hazel nut, he says, and puts it into his mouth.

Why, I don't understand it all, exclaims MOTHER. I didn't put any hazel nuts in the plum pudding. Who ever heard of such a thing! Children, have you found any in yours?

Yes, says GERTRUDE.

I've had two, says WALTER.

Mother has been looking carefully at the pudding on her plate. I declare, you're right, she says. Here's one in mine. She eats it. They are very good nuts, too; but how they ever got into the pudding is a mystery.

During this last speech the lid of the wood box has been pushed up, showing the two brownies, sitting up in the box, and also the top of the clothes basket, showing the fairies, looking out from the basket.

Walter happens to catch sight of the brownies in the wood box. He starts up from his chair, and, pointing toward the wood box, cries, There they are!

What? asks FATHER, looking in the direction to which Walter points.

The brownies, cries WALTER. See! In the wood box.

I don't see anything, says FATHER, except that someone has left the lid of the wood box open.

Oh, and the fairies, cries GERTRUDE, pointing toward the clothes basket. There they are. I see them.

MOTHER turns around to look, and then says to Gertrude. There's nothing there, my dear.

Oh, but there is, GERTRUDE declares. They are in the basket.

Everybody stands up. Gertrude and Walter come around from behind the table, and look at the fairies and brownies, but they don't go very close to them, because they are just a little bit scared. At the same time, Father begins to act rather queerly, looking down at the floor, and keeping himself up by holding onto the table. Now he goes down on his hands and knees near the end of the table.

Why, James, exclaims MOTHER, what are you doing? How queerly you are acting.

FATHER gets up again, as though by a great effort. I don't know what is the matter, he says: But I have the funniest sort of feeling. It seems as though I should just have to get down on the floor and crawl under the table.

Well, that's queer, says MOTHER. Do you know, I begin to feel the same way myself.

So do I, says GRANDMOTHER.

So do I, says GRANDFATHER.

It's perfectly absurd the way I seem to want to crawl under the table, FATHER says, and his knees keep bending under him.

But you're surely not going to do it, cries MOTHER.

Oh, no FATHER answers, I'm not going to do it. But all the same he goes down on his knees again.

But you are doing it, cries MOTHER.

Well, I can't help it, shouts FATHER. Here goes. Watch me come out at the other end.

If he goes, I've got to follow, says MOTHER, and she gets down on her hands and knees behind him.

So have I, says GRANDFATHER, and he kneels down behind Mother.

And I, says GRANDMOTHER, and she kneels behind Grandfather.

Then, close behind one another, they go under the table, and when they come out at the other end, Father and Grandfather have turned into little boys, and Mother and Grandmother have turned into little girls. While this is happening the brownies and fairies come out of the box and basket.

Oh, jolly! *cries* WALTER. Is this you, grandfather? *He takes hold of hands with the little boy that Grandfather has turned into, and swings him around in a circle.*

Oh, mother, *cries* GERTRUDE *to one of the little girls, hugging her,* how darling you are. Isn't this fun?

Let's all play some game together, *proposes* WALTER.

"London Bridge," shall we play that? GERTRUDE *suggests. The others all clap their hands; so she goes on. She says,* Walter, you and I will be the bridge. What shall we choose? *They whisper together.*

Then the game is played in the usual way. Each captive is offered a choice between "plum pudding" (that is Gertrude's side) and "ice cream" (that is Walter's side). At the very moment when the tug-of-war is about to begin, the outside door opens, and in comes Santa Claus. At once, they all leave their games, and gather around him.

Oh, Santa Claus, *cries* WALTER, have you come to play with us?

How can I play with you? *answers* SANTA CLAUS. I'm far too big, and far, far too old. *One of the fairies has gone to the table, and gotten a plate of plum pudding, which she now offers to Santa Claus.* What's this? *he asks.* Plum pudding? Well, I never could resist that. *He begins to eat it.* This surely is a first-class pudding. *He takes another spoonful.* Why, what's this? A nut in the pudding? A hazel-nut! *He stops short, and holds the plate away from him.* A hazel nut! *he exclaims again.* I declare, I'd clean forgotten all about that. And now I've gone and eaten one. Goodness! Is it going to work, I wonder. *He puts the plate down on the table.* Yes, I feel it coming. Yes, it's come. I've just got to crawl under that table. Get out of the way there. I've got to do it. It's no use trying not to.

The children, the brownies, and the fairies are all delighted, and laugh, and dance up and down, and clap their hands.

WALTER *cries out,* Go on, Santa. You'll make a jolly boy.

Down goes Santa Claus on his hands and knees, and crawls under the table. When he comes out on the other end, he is a little roley poley boy, smaller and fatter than any of the others, and dressed in white with red trimmings. All the others join hands with him in a circle, and they swing around gleefully.

Now for a game of "Follow my leader," *shouts* WALTER. I'll be leader; come after me.

Off Walter starts around the room, the others following, first Gertrude, then the brownies and the fairies, then the others, with Santa Claus bringing up the rear. They go over the wood box, onto a chair and down again, and at last Walter dives under the table, in the opposite direction to that in which the magic change was made. The children, the brownies, and the fairies go through without any change, of course, but the other five all come out in their original form. They stand up straightening their clothes, Mother and Grandmother setting their hair to rights. Meantime, while the children are occupied watching the transformations of their parents and grandparents, the brownies and fairies go back into the box and basket, and pull the lids down after them.

I'm all out of breath, *exclaims* FATHER, *panting.*

So am I, *says* GRANDMOTHER; but what fun it was.

I wouldn't have missed it for a thousand dollars, MOTHER *declares.*

Nor I, *echoes* GRANDFATHER. Even now, although I've got my old body back again, I declare I feel as young as a boy inside.

Oh, Santa Claus, *cries* GERTRUDE, you were the dearest, funniest little boy I ever saw. It just made me laugh to look at you.

Hush! *says* SANTA CLAUS, *looking cautiously over his shoulder,* I hope you won't let any one know how foolish I looked and acted. What would people say, if they heard that a man hundreds of years old like me, has been romping around that way?

Why, Santa Claus, *says* WALTER, everybody would think it was fine.

Do you think so? *asks* SANTA CLAUS, *looking around from one to the other.*

Of course, they would, *answers* FATHER. The fact is they'd love you all the more for it, if that's possible.

Dear Santa Claus, you don't mind my laughing at you, do you? *says* GERTRUDE; because you were funny, you know.

Well—no—I guess I don't mind much, SANTA CLAUS answers. In fact, the more I think of it, the more I think myself that it was funny. Ho! Ho! Ho! Only so high *(he measures the height with his hand)* and as fat as butter. Ho! Ho! Ho! *He goes off into a roar of laughter, and everybody else begins laughing, and they laugh more and more, until they have to lean up against the wall and the table, and wipe their eyes.*

When the laughing has stopped, SANTA CLAUS *says,* There's only one person I don't believe I can quite forgive, and that's the sly puss of a fairy, who gave me the plum pudding. She knew what would happen well enough. Where is she? *He looks around for her.* Why, she's gone.

So she has, *says* GERTRUDE, *looking around.* They've both gone.

And the brownies, too, *says* WALTER.

And I must be going this very minute, *exclaims* SANTA CLAUS. Goodness knows how late it is. *He goes toward the door.* Good-bye, everybody. Good-bye till next Christmas. *Just at the door he turns, and says,* By the way, I've got some more of those hazel nuts at home. What do you think I'd better do with them?

Santa Claus, *says* GRANDMOTHER, bring them with you next Christmas, and let's do it all over again.

Shall I? *asks* SANTA CLAUS, *looking around at them all.*

Yes, yes, *they* ALL *cry.*

It's a bargain, says SANTA CLAUS. Don't forget. Next Christmas. Good-bye. *He opens the door to go out.*

Good-bye till next Christmas, *they* ALL *call after him, and they wave their hands to him as the Curtain closes.*

And this is the end of the Play.

The End